Li

GW01458237

Rachel Stevens

BookLeaf
Publishing

Limbo © 2022 Rachel Stevens

All rights reserved.

Rachel Stevens asserts the moral right to be identified as author of this work.

Presentation by *BookLeaf Publishing*

Web: www.bookleafpub.com

E-mail: info@bookleafpub.com

ISBN: 9789357616669

First edition 2022

To my children, my mum, dad(s), my siblings, my cat and everyone in between.

ACKNOWLEDGEMENT

For those who have crushed me and broken me down and (most of all) for those fantastic people who have picked up the pieces.

Sometimes they are the same people.

PREFACE

Here lies: no lies.

Bathtub

I'm in a bathroom with no windows.
The plastic bathtub against my back.
It gives a feeling of great solace.
From dreaded things which may attack.

I'm slowly sinking under, but I feel such peace
surround me.
Water rocking side to side, reminiscent of the
sea.

I'm in a bathroom with a window.
The plastic bathtub against my knees.
It props me up and spits me out.
And there's no time to flee.

I'm quickly sinking under, and I feel no peace
around.
Water rocking side to side and crashing to the
ground.

The Unbearable Weight of Silence

This life it seems impossible.
This life is terribly fierce.
This life cannot be bearable.
This face is full of tears.

I'm wringing out whole towels.
And fighting to stay still.
This feeling lasts several hours.
And I've yet to reach the hill.

There are so many different things that I could
say.

But I didn't say them yesterday and I won't say
them today.

Flying

You float across the road as if…
As if you've seen the most.
Delightful thing upon tarmac…
And sometimes with bare toes.

With elation you glide from the steps of the
station.
Right under my nose.

I wish you were in front of my nose.

The one I cherish most.
I am right in front of his nose.

You

I want to know the you I once saw.
Standing against the shopping wall.
I see you out there, clear as ice.
Sitting on the grandest steps.

One night not long ago, sung you.
A song so precious, you plucking dude.
I hear you out there, clear as ice.
Sitting in the loudest house.

I want to know the you I saw.

You have such a gift for hiding yourself from
me.

Help

Help is at hand, old thing.
I'll listen to you whilst you balk.
A hand is here for you to hold.
An ear, so you can talk.

Help is here, young thing.
To listen to your cries.
As you talk of many dreadful things.
And take me by surprise.

With your resolve and clarity.
You teach me things I could not see.

Before I go, do you need more?
I'm here with you as you vent.
I'm with you and listening here tonight.
About how you're scared or can't pay the rent.

Help is at hand, middle thing.
I know things feel impossible now.
You're truly an inspiration, you are.
And you'll get there, I mean it, somehow.

With your resilience, your words.
You teach me things I haven't heard.
Thank you.

Rambling on

Above hills and mountaintops, I stop.
Admire the view on the other side.
And when you're in the view, it's true.
You appreciate wonders with each new stride.

With you sat inside this backpack, I track.
How many hills we've climbed together.
Your little face is peeking out and about.
We go trekking whatever the weather.

Amongst friends with young, we're flung.
Into adventures sweet (not) sour.
Climbing over styles, over miles.
And resting in the final hour.

Furry familiar

You're furry familiar.
As I face my very darkest hour.
You're faintly familiar.
As I look outwards for half an hour.

You're feeling familiar.
When the light turns every shade of sour.
You're very familiar.
Like the feeling when you want to cower.

You're my furry familiar.
And I see you in the day and night.
You're my sudden companion.
Please stay with me whilst I tremble.

You see, I'm not fierce, or bold, or anything like you.
With your flakes of gold and your autumn hue.

Please stay with me for half an hour.
Please stay with me for half an hour.

Profanities

As notes are ringing in my ear.
You're not here.

As I face the very thing I fear.
You're not here.

When I tend to every other thing.
You're not here.

As I mutter out profanities.
You're not here.

As I lose my very sanity.
You're not here.

As you lose your own humanity.

You're there.

Tethered

My arms against my legs they feel,
All scrunched up and stuck.
I dream of being light as solid smoke,
Instead of all screwed up and stuck.

My back is burning holes into the plaster of the
wall.
And I feel lost and empty if I feel anything at all.

My legs beneath my arms they seem,
Tethered to the ground.
Attached by some tremendous beam,
And rooted to the ground.

Books on a Box

A pile of books on a box.
Are imploring me to read them.
They sit and sigh inside.
Start calling me to read them.

The teetering pile remains.
Waiting for a second look.
Clinging on for dear life.
And saving floor space.

When I open them.
Who can tell?
They're just sitting there.
And they smell.

But it's not a bad scent, you understand.
They're fragrant, glorious, and yet, getting out
of hand.

This teetering pile keeps growing and I smile.
I'll get around to reading them once in a while.

Work

You have your day job and your side job.
Your little hustle pays the rent.
Your day job has you covered.
So other funds they can be spent.

You have your main job and your half job.
Your side hustle is so sweet.
It allows you to show your creative side.
And provides food you so greedily eat.

Your day job and your night job.
Both fulfil a different need.
You have your day job and your night job.
And your all-consuming greed.

Pressure

Teasing time, when facing your crime.
Forgetting the saviour,
Who taught you a sublime.
Way through life and the trials it brings.
Holding so tightly to loosely-bound strings.

(Fate holds us all in its tightly-wound claw).

Awake, yet frozen, this fire burns fierce.
Leaving the ember aglow many years.
Along this line, descendants they pass.
Reaching the pinnacle and joys of their past.

(I'm fearing it will not have enough and want
more).

Tearing through life, not a moment to spare.
Wasting our promises without a care.
This isn't goodbye and it isn't farewell.
It's damning you to eternity in some kind of hell.

(Fate holds us all in its tightly-wound claw.
I'm fearing it will not have enough and want
more).

Gigging

This engaging mass of bodies,
Free from the tyres of life.
Blend together as one,
On this blissful night.

Believing their wishes to be conceived.
Knowing this evening is only growing.

Tonight is the night the angels depart.
Raring to go. For tomorrow, mayhem starts.

Tom and his friends encouraged no end.
By the swaying of arms and the clicking of
lens'.

It's not only flowers that sway in the breeze.
Hyperventilating and falling to their knees.
Every body awake and willing to listen.
Lights above and outside glisten.

Stars and a moon from many moons away.
Embracing the night and reminiscing the day.

Grin

So I tried internet dating.
And I messaged pretty boys,
But engaging messages.
Can't compete with your noise.

The noise you cause within me,
When you walk by.
And the sound of your voice,
From downstairs as I lie.

To everyone and you.
(But myself most of all).
Couldn't stand it if I told you.
And faced a fall.

My spirit is weak from rejection.
And I feel lost at sea.
And I only feel calm.
When you're there talking to me.

About anything sweetheart.
Anything at all.
The state of the world.
Or various squash balls.

About music or love online.
And oh, those bike rides in the sun.
There is nothing better than you my dear.
No activity more fun.

Then talking and walking.
And time with you.

Or even just at home.
Fighting over Mario.
Or setting the world to rights.
On one of our nights.

In which everyone intervenes.
And everyone sees.
But not a single person understands.
That I want you in my lands.

Not in a crude way.
Just plain and simple. Duvet.
You and me, under sheets.
Forever talking. Eyes as one.

You are one charming boy.
Please catch me, smiling.
Happy to be your girl.
With a grin the size of the world.

At Last

We frolic across the grass.
And we, laugh and laugh and laugh.
Talk about some crazy things.
And then, follow a different path.

Drinking fizzy drinks and then,
Thinking funny thinks.
We dance around the universe,
And find our missing links.

The (not so great) Depression

Oppressive black heart attack, why do you
scare?
I'm barely breathing, do you even care?
Doom is approaching, I sense your wrath.
And feel the energy as you destroy your path.

Melting all obstacles, building your way.
I will surely face you one terrible day.

I cry out in pain as you smother my mind.
Try to escape but you leave me blind.
Unsure of my fate or how to find my way.
Maybe I'll scare you to death one day.

Who am I kidding?
It's you who's in charge.
A monster, a savage, a beast is at large.

But I don't fear you anymore.
So don't come knocking.
I'm time-poor.

The Future

It was the best of days.
It was the worst of days.
For someone so small, you test my patience in
untold ways.

Yet I love you so fiercely.
I protect you so fiercely.
And I struggle in feeling so fierce myself.

Feeling such a bad parent.
Struggling to hold in my temper.
Not always talking to you in the calmest, best
tone.

Having to constantly wrestle with you over
every decision.
Until I feel stress making a home for itself in my
bones.

Might go into premature labour with the strain
of it all.
But oh how I love you, boy.
You are so small.
But so smart and switched on.

We're trying to teach you it all.
When we don't even know how to live ourselves.
You're precious and a pain in the arse of our
world.
Lovely little chap.

What will the future unfurl?

Have a Wonderful Tomorrow

How is your recital going?
Did you have a good evening dear?
Did you meet up with your friends?
Did they invite your for a beer?

Are you happy where you are?
Physically and in life.
Do you wish you had a girlfriend?
And will you ever have a wife?

Do you think about me sometimes?
In that way.
And do you recall that summer's day?

When we cycled to Portland.
And wobbled our way back.

When we fought over Donkey Kong.
And when it was just us in the house.

Do you remember?
Do you wish you were with me?
Do you want to travel the world some more?
Do I want you to be happy?
Always.

Bright

You're rolling around on the floor, young one.
You're chattering in your own way.
Rushing towards the door, young one.
And making your own special way.

You're standing up for yourself, little one.
You're wandering all around.
Running, then tripping, tiny little one.
And creating your own sound.

You're bigger than yesterday, sweet one.
You're growing every day.
Out into the world, sweet one.
For it to lead you astray.

You're made of stronger stuff, my girl.
Your brother, he is too.
I wish I could protect you forever my guys.
But the world will do as it will.

When the cows come to roost

When the cows come to roost,
(As I know they will).
I'll see you striding down the meandering hill.

And when the chickens come to moo,
(As I know they do).
I'll hear you saying something that isn't true.

Hope

When I see your beaming eyes. There's hope.
When you laugh as all else cries. There's hope.
Treading out into the world. With hope.
You're the only things that matter.

As you run and jump so high. I cope.
And even when you say goodbye. I cope.
Trekking out into the wild. I cope.
You're off to face the world. With hope.

Milton Keynes UK
Ingram Content Group UK Ltd.
UKHW020655200923
429044UK00015B/454

9 789357 616669